for Roland & Anna,
with good wishes always -
Peter Dent 6. iv. 19

A Wind-Up Collider

Peter Dent

A Wind-Up Collider

Shearsman Books

First published in the United Kingdom in 2019 by
Shearsman Books
50 Westons Hill Drive
Emersons Green
BRISTOL
BS16 7DF

Shearsman Books Ltd Registered Office
30–31 St. James Place, Mangotsfield, Bristol BS16 9JB
(this address not for correspondence)

www.shearsman.com

ISBN 978-1-84861-666-0

WITH THANKS TO THE EDITORS OF

HQ Poetry Magazine, *International Times*, *Stride* and *Tears in the
Fence*, where some of these pieces made their first appearance.
Others were included in *A Festschrift for Tony Frazer* (online), 'The
Revival of the Inspectorate for Everything' (Treadmill Editions) and
'The First Ghost Train out of Nowhere' (Hole-and-Corner Press).

Special thanks to Georgie and Stephen, for weathering my
various absences – notably, in the mind and study. Also, to
Rupert Loydell, for keeping me up to speed with upheavals,
marvellous and other, in the arts.

CONTENTS

One
A Surrogate Dream

Two
A Broken Angel or A Bundle of Straws

Here I come, the invisible man, perhaps employed
by a Great Memory to live right now. And I am driving past

the locked-up white church – a wooden saint is standing in there
smiling, helpless, as if they had taken away his glasses

Tomas Tranströmer, 'December Evening 1972'
(translated by Robin Fulton)

One

A SURROGATE DREAM

DEWDROPS AND THE OUT-OF-BODY EXPERIENCE

By late Autumn we were piling into our margins and looking
through wardrobes for heavies: this sounds chaotic.   It is.
A conceit: a refusal to mourn one another's passing or, as it
turned out, more.   I had to wonder why people insisted on
blocking the flat entrance with mountain bikes and boots.   I
was not disposed to going out less clad than those who'd
been in regular contact with their feelings and who thought
being ahead of the game meant you'd get both hot water
and the soap – there wasn't much to say about the text.   By
removing commas you could cram more in and finish up
with heaps more energy than you'd get by talking the hind
leg off an energy company's infatuated answer machine.   It
gave me time to weep for all those ghosts that failed me in
my historic prime, and yank on an extra 100% nylon layer.

THE UNLIKELY

Adult nights draw in – and deer tread so softly, I cannot, even at this point in my life, speak of leaves or close my eyes and imagine gold.   I once confided in my mother, saying I would see to everything, knowing my mind was grounded in half a dozen miracles of presence.   As befits, I beware mildness like the plague.   Too few of my companions made it this far, no-one hinted he'd seen it coming.   Leaves spiralling to the ground.   Late migrants worrying at the light and cherished reserves – I'm still on someone nameless's payroll, wondering for how long: at a certain age, labyrinths and mothers come into their own.   My evening schedules beg to be rearranged.

WHAT'S ON

Stuffed birds in cases – rainbow-coloured models from some design course sporting antique poses. A guide usually to show you the ruins. The evocative unnerving dark-framed photographs of the person you were prior to a few drinks and accompanying enlightenment, when the past was sold off as scrap and you could pick up moon shot mementoes for less than a pound. If only you'd asked nicely, they might have treated you to a warmed-up old classic say Horace – just one of the jokers that could do it backwards. This, scarily, is a live museum. Everything updated and the bushy-tailed backstory yours to keep; the old have had it, O.K., kids rule.

DAY CARE

for Colin Oliver

You've probably seen it – a blackbird, half-awake, sitting (or
rather, propping himself) on the wall, one wing extended, at
a comfortable angle to the sun.   Lots of things there are that
don't merit a mention.   I look across the road to Spar – the
man outside, unhitching his dog as a girl runs past.   The day
already running thick with event and associated (I suppose
they are?) modern myths – which, of course, I believe in, as
everything and even nothing wears on.   The cosmos fading.
After all, it's mid-October, last night was cold – Tomasz says
+1° (stress on the plus – as if we may well have been lucky?).
And there's a cyclist down from the hill: more speed than he
knows what to do with, at least in one kind of way, he's fine.

TOO CLOSE TO THE SUN

Mercury, for one, could do with a pair of shades, she said,
tilting her head back.   Could I see where this was leading?
Of course I couldn't!   You know, orbits are running rings
around us, she went on.   I decided not to respond,
but spent the next eight hours off air – not adrift and not
hurrying back to base.   She was all about her business:
I was predictably obtuse, offering neither wise words nor
glimpses of sentience – too much has crashed and burned.
I can't imagine a life so realised there is nothing I'd want
more, but a half-moon to look up to and beam me down.

A POWER OF GOOD

They have recommended a book of non-specific no-go areas
for controlled investigation.   Of all that ails thee, think not
once but again and again and be nothing if not healed – the
price of poverty is pain.   Life is both occasional and perfect,
as your sun shines, so let it.   Continuous reinvention sounds
more like politics than it should and the P.M. has a shedload
of explaining to do.   Which leads me to an embassy I shall
not name that has windows looking in too many directions:
one cannot, excuse me, bare all.   Many fine things there are
that need to be everything or else – that they help the world
go round is the theory.   My suspicions are a battleground.
It's so crowded one can scarcely breathe.   Come all ye who.

TO THIS DAY

It was one tactile blunder after another.   He was but a part-time pioneer of the night, scavenging like a bear among bins for nigh on 3 weeks unemptied of everything he held dear and in suspension.   Whilst he felt himself to be far from diminished, he wasn't one to shape a controlling narrative. Dark rain fell, and, in the manner of the unconvicted, he was never inside for acts of contrition.   Falling, not something to grow on trees, was the orchard's only deception.   His apples being of a distinctly mild demeanour and delight. What touched him greatly was the recognition he was the only story with a character to play up to.   Till the school-bell rang, he'd be the bravest savage and every hunter's kill.

BEHIND CLOSED DOORS

There are photographs and a wodge of jottings.   I've tried to
question the ownership and been greeted by disbelief.   The
cast assemble in locations that cannot, in anyone's good book,
be believed.   Because words choose their moment doesn't
mean there's ice on their wings – no, they are as personal as a
peacock's roundels or a baby's ears.   The invitation remains,
seven day opening was always the case, where have you been?
They, the big questions, elicit responses both grave and comic
and my impulse – if not yours – is to drain them of their life-
blood like any good vampire.   Whatever terrifies or has you
wiping away the tears goes into the mix: who can anyone be?

ACTIVISM AS YOU LIKE IT

The time is now. Correction: then. I'm beginning to get the
hang of *some* of the words – I do it carefully, I do it dodging
security and diving down steps into my underground of jazzy
dreams. See the colours, listen to the sounds. Dickens kept
me in the dark for so long, I got to read without a torch. I'll
be in my element come Midsummer. Whatever's on the wall
will keep me posted: the barricades not a problem as long as
I can spell 'Exchequer' without paying over the odds – try me!

A TRIFLE UNREAD   *for David Caddy*

Who shall we be and when might we become them?   That
becoming and the combination of high security and catac-
lysm that keeps us in order – or in a state of terror.   We've
purchased certain freedoms, haven't we?   But not enough
to cut our ties!   Crevasses, sink holes, quicksands, craters.
If it's a metaphor you're after and a theatre to show it off in,
use the Job Centre.   Serious 'business' happens sotto voce
when nothing's on in the window – don't talk to me about
bloody aftermaths.   The Globe has seen it all.   I've stood
beside a pillar and watched the best and worst of them fall.
Deliverance has come, if it has come, at a cost: gunpowder
being the least of it.   Love's too often cut us to the quick.
I'll be what I want to be.   To hell with it, I've had enough.

SPELL IT YOUR WAY

Places at the top table don't come up so often you get to pick and choose.   I spelled it my way with an extra 'o' – it was that arresting.   Space junk is so far away, it's out of mind and I look up only when I have to, which is, essentially, when I first leave the hostelry, dreaming through my handbook of creative desire.   As it stands, I rival CGI for faking up my identity and flirting with the world.   The world has no idea that angelic forces are playing their part.   If it does, then I'm out of a job. Abandonment is naturally what you make of it and I mightn't.

FLOCK WALLPAPER

Flying ducks, antimacassars, artex and hostess trolleys.   The
day before yesterday, a government of fools, the first person
on the moon and the starry end of all beginnings, which you
fall for, playing one hour off against another.   Coming back
when someone says your mother's calling, then an 8hr sleep
punctuated by trains, bells, by a barking dog (occasionally a
fox), by the alarm that'll need rewinding.   Or tomorrow may
never arrive, the way that you dream it and every dream with
threads attached for pulling at absentmindedly, angrily, what-
ever.   Yet another parquet floor to shine.   Things like this
that keep turning up, when, in the run of things, you'd rather
they didn't – what do you do, I'm listening, send them back?

SPACES TO KILL   *for Yann and Ann Lovelock*

According to the gospel, things came as no surprise.   They'd
been foretold.   These days the focus group does something
similar, but who asks now after a) armageddon or b) the kind
of settled consumer friendly life they'd planned for in the first
place?   Here then is another windswept corner of the mind.
Ball park figures just out of town, something to look at when
the scenery's not so rosy.   'Reliquary for a Day' is the perfect
programme to miss if it weren't around – and you constantly
aren't.   Too busy swapping goodies at a 'safe place', sharing
disinformation.   Watchers, one and all, happy as Larry in the
desert, white robed, holier than thou, scared only of shadows.

TOURING WITH BIG BEASTS

Deskill, reanimate as many dead-and-alive tracks as you can
think of, tear out the vocal and replace with a synth that's
seen better days, précis all the lyrics right down to a phrase
a corpse might remember, sporting replica scars, and make
that the title, soon as whenever take it on the road that's no
place to be in one's right mind, back to studio, there trash
the original rhythm and play it backward the way it clearly
demanded, leaving lacunae intact, then plugging in epitaphs
to yourself and all who helped you become the ghost you
almost became and were so glad you didn't, adding wobbly
bells and an extended, fading whisshh of air – to finish us
off, like you would on a day you were never up for – the
puppets that are the band disjointed, hanging from strings.

THE UNEXPECTED

She wanted, badly, to enlarge her appeal.　Things grew tense
as circumstances permitted – she ran with the most violent
story you could possibly imagine, wolves too.　I think it takes
one to know one, which leaves me totally without her mind.
No title to go on, she single-handedly set up camp on the
veldt and began work on her masterpiece.　She played hero
and villain – don't tell me she was suited – and packed in
every last drop of vitriol to keep out the cold.　On her return I
found her bearable only a sentence at a time – night sweats
are now a thing of the past.　I walk the streets and grieve.
This won't be the last time, her face leaping out of the screen.

SPELLBOUND

for John Riley

Another week has come and gone.   Memory has white space
too, hasn't it?   About some of it, I can tell you nothing, which
leaves a bitter-sweet taste in the mouth – invention may like
to fill the gap.   Dramatis personae, once-real or never.   A lot
of happening.   Some day love will crowd the set.   We'll all
know where we stand.   Long-term liberties can't always cope.
Remember those monks who do not speak; time trying to pin
each edgy history to the ground.   My memoir's a night club
of too much and far too little.   I feel like a heartache in flight.

GAMEKEEPERS AND CROWS *for Harry Guest*

My tutorial was overcrowded. Voices overheard. Some of
them overhead. We went, as was our wont, from one thing
to another – deliverance via an exit lit up in green with a veil
you could tear away. Intrigue lay like sunset, ripplets over a
pool. I quoted Erasmus, requiring stamina (and not just on
my part) and swift concessions from everybody concerning
'impartiality', also 'Cynthia' (Propertius, his elegies) in reality
Hostia. She couldn't help it, it was her eyes that did it: bad
moons rising, then, as happens, bad luck. But, he loved his
Virgil and, on a braver day, they died: I put it down to paper.

'STEAL AWAY'

I was backing myself.   To the very end.   If nothing comes
of it, why interfere?   If I thought I recognised myself in the
mirror, it was all I had to go on.   My assistant was off for
the day, there was no-one else to turn to.   It wouldn't be the
first time I'd doctored an aphorism, but it might be the last.
Everything, and I'm thinking of sunshine, traffic noise and
the water fountain, kept me on my toes.   An everyday case
– that's all it was.   No bloodstains on the carpet, nothing
but coffee and crumbs.   I looked at the screen, which clued
me in to what came next.   I sat waiting what seemed like
hours.   I knew I could fix an outcome, but if I can't believe
it, I need proper reassurance.   I need others as much as you.

ONE THING AFTER ANOTHER *for Alan Baker*

A succession of e.g. coincidences.   Taking up an intellectual
position on the basis of one good turn deserves another.   I'd
been the recipient of a prize for flying in the face of.   My
glider buffeted by icy winds, guess-who singing at the top of
his voice when all seemed lost.   I read my instruments like a
paper on The Perks of Free Will.   Was it kind to shed light
on the motivations of art?   Or, on a dire Sunday in August,
put all conceptions of time to the sword?   Grief.   You have
to believe in something?   Man exists to go with whatever a
thermal has to offer and then do the other.   Man 'exists'.   I
don't doubt that, just after take-off, the sky's complicit.   I'm
happy to remember Kiefer's lead aeroplanes and abstract the
impact for a Big Book of Conviction, maybe a way of life.

CHAOS PARTY (THE ESTABLISHED ORDER)

A break in the weather often prompts a blizzard of notes,
encouraging guesswork as well as shortness of breath – if
I hadn't told you, would you have known?   Not saying so
was actually deliberate.   The last doctor to check me over
had long since dispensed with his instruments.   He relied
entirely on interrogation, being brutal with both the truth
and his personal eschatology (think climaxes).   I began
to suffer spasms & gyrations (not unlike those on a dance
floor?) – the leftovers of a hung-over mind?   I felt it right
across the system.   Light hung about me, brilliant as the
essay I'd written and handed in – turned down flat by an
editor with a broken hand.   But, he was wincing and gas-
ping more than I was.   I gave him 48 hrs to think about it,
but he said he couldn't go back.   I guess, in an inclement
kind of way, both of us were (till who knows when & why)
'semi-retired'.   There was little more on our minds than
the dance.   So the band promised to dedicate a lament.

FRENETICS

A day humouring your mentor is a day misspent.   It's my own
decision to nurse a rumour and engineer a ploughshare.   I
expect a living, but don't we all?   Lies all told are a
monument to our mystery: what we see in others is
probably twice what we see in ourselves, don't underestimate.
Any story on a good day fires a song worth singing
for your supper.   Spit it out.   You were a vagrant,
you carried clouds of anything.   Saddlebags stuffed with life.
But clarity?   I love a cloud with a conscience, I will hear it out.

STORY FOR THE FIRST THURSDAY IN OCTOBER

The tree lasted so long, I can't remember not seeing it, but then I did – my script gives a first-hand account of its first flowering, so I must have been there.   Not a quotation or a surrogate dream: barbed wire came into its own in WW1. There were too few trees to hide behind.   Most of them broken.   My father was one that took a ricochet and I think the testimony of many such survive in Ypres and beyond.   It's just that a family tree has names you can hold on to and others that can't bear the reading.   This is not as difficult as it seems – but I can see what you're thinking.

TAKING FOR GRANTED   *for Roland and Anna John*

There is no substitute for a river it's hard not to fall into.   A
'warm water port' (see politics) is no more than a bucket of
idle dreams you'd better not get into or secretly condone: my
uncle held up two shipmates when the ship went down – till
he could do it no longer.   It was an article in the daily.   A
fact, and as big as it gets.   Essentially, we're in a stable, self-
healing world (see Gaia) we're given to ignore or play up
to.   One day we'll all be holding on.   And sooner than we'd
like.   Colours matter that float agreeably anywhere between
green, blue and grey.   Much of the life I've led has been about
allegation and counter-allegation.   Most of the books I read
I question: fish swim with eyes wide open, is there any doubt?

DISSEMBLING (A LIFE)

I headed off downstairs at a rate I wouldn't want critics to
calculate – necessity was, not for the first time, my mother.
The maid received a sentence commensurate with her role
in the story.   Despite her assurances, revolution was in its
infancy, the nursery had plans of its own.   Watchful eyes
were the property of nobody as far as I could see.   The C
in conservative stood for capital or a walk in the park.   By
the time I had committed, thirty years had passed and the
way the game was played meant closing ranks.   All sides
had sustained casualties – the rocking horse was chipped
and faded – balance wasn't in it.   Plotting a course made
me exactly what I am; meddling will see me pay the price!
If I step on it, I can print off a form showing that not only
was I nowhere near, the villain was a journo I'd never met.

MISSING THE POINT

I've been in a hostel, slept in an air-raid shelter and a tent.
My great-great-grandfather-in-law slept under a hedge.
One night he forgot his bike and had to go back next day
to pick it up from the publican.   I admit, the second half
of that is part-invention, but it's not untrue.   Views over
the city take in skyscrapers (U.K. sort), shops, cathedrals
and a band of frozen refugees.   A wrecking ball's not for
setting any kind of precedent – let's not do people down.

VOICING CHAOS

Interference, bad reception?   If I don't take myself to spots
I've carefully calculated, it's anyone's guess where the next
flare-up's going to be.   'Station Zero', as a name, will be
effectively scrubbed and switched to a place near you.   Or
me.   Do bullets and streams of exhausted marchers matter,
if they're confined to the background?   You tell me if the
knight about to mount his charger ever looks back at her
and bothers to wave – whichever way, her handkerchief will
be out.   I ought to know better, but I keep on listening,
even when the song is done.   Something in the sky, then?

FAIRYTALE EXISTENCE

I deceive myself, you regiment yourself into tight corners.   As
a psychiatrist experiments with minds, so creativity comes into
its own.   Do you remember privacy?   A campus novel from
1958 is like the red-headed mistress you don't have now, but
had at the time.   If the years 1958 – 1972 mean nothing, then
I've been living in a fog.   Don't get me wrong, I apportion no
blame whatsoever.   Other years are dogged enough to chew
over both the facts *and* fancies of your indelible case.   Look,
here's one cliché and there's another.   The coffee cup and its
grouts have already colonised continents: I drink to the time
tales come over so bittersweet, so true, I cannot make you up.

THE WAYSIDE, THE WAXWORKS
AND THE PRINTSHOP *for Cathy Hales*

In this lifetime of leaking secrets, no centres of artifice and
virtual freedom remained sacrosanct: the new cult groups
hell-bent on playing their hearts out while blasted heaths
east of Berlin reckoned on this kind of thing overstaying
at home.   Buttered crumpets at the fireside, daughters of
a family friend upended in the marriage stakes: take these
plastic bags for your possessions – files once kept holed
up in the oak trees of unfamiliar forests nobody cared to
name.   Privacy alongside bouts of incipient madness, the
next best thing.   How minimal was the coverage!   A few
nights' footage, a bit of that word on the street blown here
and there by the wind ....   Few real secrets, and like burnt
chestnuts, good (almost too good) to give away.   Or so
we thought – Operation 'Swansong': whistling in the dark.

WARRING AGAINST THE ODDS

Here I was guiding an expedition (and just listen to the date: 1938), little knowing there'd be talk of actual force.   Had I checked the indictments against known – I repeat known – offenders, we'd have seen less one-upmanship and more anonymity.   I can't picture anyone getting down on their hands and knees and drawing lines across Europe.   Flowers and graves only too anxious to keep us in the Land of Nod. I'll hand over all of my contributions willingly, if they're worthy of a place that's kind: lavish upon me what you will. It's another expedition now – I won't be talking about force.

SAMPLING ERROR

What about the content?   How can I excise alarmist head-
lines if the vaccine's still too dear to prescribe?   What kind
of patient takes it upon himself/herself to reject the next best
thing and blame it on the book of the film?   Where the lead's
your trading partner and your mouse has a mind of its own –
laying down stingers for what's coming up?   Will the auction
benefit more from rigging, if the cast forget their words?
Ideologically, comedy is ever in the right place – people in
the ministry have as much idea of the economy as slapstick
can fight a war.   The papers have their cake and eat it.   I've
lived too long in expectation of hope cheering you all up.
I could do it myself – if asked – by numbers up to a point.

GOLD DUST

Whether to feel lonely or not is always the problem. You
know the correct answer but know nothing about the time
it takes to assemble, then massage the facts – I've put more
theories to bed than anyone I know, though that involves
a bit of guesswork.   Visions that disturb are ten a penny.
A change in one's appetite ranks alongside certain national
myths as the harbinger of madness to come.   'Hereabouts'
is a very bad place, but the council tax is, or should be, the
least of my worries; being on my own isn't so much a trial
as facing the judge.   I grew up thinking all of it was real.

SNUFFING OUT FIRES

for Alan Halsey

Today the light is unremittingly indigo: being aware of change
and doing nothing to mitigate it is the penultimate sin, but
some decision-making bodies go for the easy option (isn't that
what you'd expect in places of correction?).   It occurs to me,
I don't always know when cynicism and the like start sweet-
talking my persona.   What is to be believed when you tell
me the front-runner for the award spoke of me in such kindly
terms that two or three in the audience gasped and searched
their pockets for small change, a torch (the lights were too
dim to read a mind) and their little book of sighs.   Not being
privy to their identity or the hazards involved, I promised
vehemently to keep a civil tongue in my head, if that's what
it takes to see a way through.   Microbial clouds make fools
of us all, so I reckon, but, then, we're all in them together.   A
penny for your thoughts (let's not end it with a car crash)?
Whatever you're counting out, I'll colour in.   At any rate (0
to 60, give or take), I remember pink and slate grey, white and
blushes of blue – my daybook's heaving with plans for the sky.

DIVIDED ISSUES   *i.m. William Cookson*

This is a companion piece to my last, if you can locate it.   The
café, at the time, was full to bursting, the waitress doing her
level best.   In a moment or two, I'll remember what you said
and paste it into the text.   What's in it for me, she asked, and
chaos picked up several unexpected nominations for the role
of 'she who succumbs' in Ionesco's 'Rhinoceros'.   Dear Daisy,
where are we now?   Like all of us, you are as make-believe
as reality.   The one who'd taken my order ran away, to pray.
We get what we want: when the play's over, we bury our dead.

I ABANDONED ALL HOPE IN THE LOOP

A xerox of the actual debriefing was left on the 2.19.   They'd
asked me questions about contacts, but I was having none of
it.   How many languages did I speak, what did I understand
by 'The Faraday Cage', 'Operation Wild Boy' etc.   Personal
integrity and gain didn't come into it – if I were a designer, a
chair would look like a chair and not a command post.   No
lights were left on but those critical to the inquiry: I wouldn't
be detained longer than necessary.   Everything I'd seen was
teetering on the edge of Perception – in secular societies, re-
deploying the past isn't unknown, but less and less is it held
in awe.   I've mercifully resolved the issue around amnesia.
You install a gatekeeper, practise your chokehold and see all
futures look the other way.   *When a train leaves, I am on it.*

ATOMIC NUMBERS   *for Mark Goodwin*

These are just thoughts.   You may get to know them.
Rather than duck out of a close reading, I'm going for
another trajectory altogether.   If we called it home,
we called it Summer and, no doubt, that's what it was.
Time raced or dragged and slot machines, for a matter
of years, played a part in it.   I was midway between
adding inches and attempting to reinstate a lost cause:
pinboard loaded with messages and nobody in when
they called.   Don't be shocked if I tell you death had
come upon us, but let's forget about that.   I stored
my pictures the way some people raid a supermarket.
Before and after a hurricane.   Often as not I'd meet
myself coming back.   Take my word for it, on a good
day (much like today) we talked the future to death.

PHOTOFIT ANYONE?

The corruption of a panel of 'expert witnesses', the overlooked
case of 'a man with a message' holed up in an embassy by
forces gathered outside and across the media …   It would be
wise to take the temperature before attempting anything from
a range of knee-jerk responses.   Pale faces pale more easily
into the background.   Visions melt faster than any ice in the
Arctic and you wonder why you, too, are not inside.   Techno-
phobes – no, I'm not one, despite what you've heard – they
might have made a difference, given any say.   These days an
eye with an iris and fingers with prints are no more than a hint
of it.   Picking you out of a crowd's a couple of clicks away.
As it is, anything you didn't say makes more sense than what
you did.   Respect, you understand, comes naturally to a head.

A FANFARE FOR CREATIVE DISORDER

Dark and mizzly, bad enough to trash a hairstyle and collide with a badly placed post.   I'm on the street and making or trying to make the best of a bad day, executing a sharp left and deftly avoiding consequences.   Politics are a gift to any comedian with mud on his boots – you know nothing if you weren't on the qui vive when steel followed coal down the plug.   Nights under streetlamps are one kind of curative: I get a better view of what they're up to when they try doctoring the masses – sweeteners, in this kind of situation, are never good for your health.   They interfere with transport between the cerebral cortex and the cerebellum.   I'd like to thank my stylist for everything he's done.   You do the best with what you've got and hope the weather lets up – grade 7 keeps most things under control.   I get to sleep at night.

RIOTS OF INFLUENCE

Yours is a credible story, do I believe it?   No, I don't.   In my
experience, finding the horse before the cart is rare enough,
but when the vehicle's packed with high explosives and cold
question marks, the whole world looks askance, i.e. the other
way.   It was as inevitable the lights would change as there'd
be a dust-up between international sensibilities.   Art feels it
like an oven, set on high, and I have five years, give or take a
dozen.   You say you're done with the mad house and ready
to return to Naturalism – at least in the foreground.   What's
in it for me? I ask and, suddenly, things aren't so clear.   My
portfolio reeks of materials dragged from nowhere you've got
a clue about: you read me no better than I read you.   A
'Life' has a life of its own, or, if found wanting, you lend one.

WHATEVER I DO

If you're a card-carrying member, it'll be me arrested for the
LCD 'beautiful idea' everyone swore they'd buy into and then,
per person (due to non-plurality), didn't.   The album treated
'concept' as other and was so aggressive toward the engineer,
The Culture re-convened in the village hall to re-introduce
water-boarding, but the music was good, in fact, frighteningly
so.   Surface water drained away immediately, thanks to its
vibrations.   Eight tracks, four each side of a big vinyl disc or
EP – chasing the same goal – abstraction via utter and totally
believable misrepresentation.   Thus, when it didn't sell out
overnight and the Health Squad asked (doorstep, no warning,
5 a.m.), 'Which one is Pink?', I, for one, didn't know where to
put myself.   Or the punctuation.   Famous occasions call on
serial killers and mad critics: my case, in the great scheme of
things, is of less than average consequence.   Loony Tunes.
Don't worry about filling in the blanks, you can use my cribs.

THE SINGER SINGS   *i.m. Ian Robinson*

The dreamer dreams; when one good turn calls for another,
it's hard to believe you're not on a loop.   Banging heads or
messing with electropop speaks to many and it's easy to see
why.   First, they tell you what's going on below the surface,
then get you to abstain from 'favourite practice'.   They are
a million miles (the politics of a new orthodoxy?) from your
taste, reverting to base instincts, group therapy and pilates.
I do care, I do want to please, but, well, insecurity lurks, as a
nymph in the greenwood tearfully explains, when you're out
of your depths.   It's not the big trees you can't see, but the
medication they dole out.   In one form or other, the song
makes my hair stand on end, I need the grace to hear it out.

THE BEST TARIFF FOR YOU

Is also the best tariff for your provider.   Systems go crazy, if
you try counting up fans in Euphoria.   I much prefer peer
reviews when a promoter can't or won't get the racket.   I
always underpay.   Also, I'm dogged enough to be absent
if local bigwigs turn up unannounced.   Robots, in a year
or 2, may well be taking thought instruction.   But it's up
to you how you play it.   I've a gut feeling, though, that
a word in their ear's worth 2 at the point of recycling: key-
change?   Make what you will of our days of thunder and
lightning – chorus, hooks and light (acoustic) engineering.
Pouring out relief like a duff dispenser when you thump it.
I want 2 rubber bands round each pile of notes + a head-
banging intro to the vaults at PanGlobal Miss Management.

FLAVOUR OF THE MONTH

Cold northerlies have seen the martins gather over rooftops. Their reach is exceeded only by nobody's grasp of market conditions. The university, as if in a daze, is developing a dumb model to suss out options. What's on offer calls for incentives. Therefore, stop backing our 'better judgment'. Quality/abundance spell out the value of anything – there's nothing now you can't get by thieving (inward investment). According to one student (studying for her Master's in Left Field Arts), a long-term dreamer's more likely to be caught up in a big domestic – it's that or face buying in essentials from those (I cannot name names) who should know better.

'WOODEN STATUE OR EURO MAKES DEBUT MINUS HEAD'

A decade, even two, in obscurity?   Not a bad thing, if I can't
be doing it.   You know what I'm like and you don't mind
saying it.   Austerity today.   Austerity tomorrow.   Treason
would be okay on an outcrop somewhere south of Greece.
But, here, the song of a crossword knows where nous can
take you.   It's all about unfilled nothings in a system no-
body gives an X for.   Borders like these, no matter how well
patrolled, leak just about anything you don't put your mind
to.   Tomorrows see you in the public eye in a twinkling.
They'll love you for your contribution to this virtual debate.
'Pincer movement cleans out trust with gleeful gambling.'
Some clues are clear: warm blue water trickles over my toes.

A TOUR OF DUTY

Money is left out with the empties.   Two steps down to
the street, and it's a scene I find ordinary enough, but
for the overturned carriage, the crisp white linen, seven-
teen boxes of papers, spelling disaster for its occupants.
Maybe, one day, there'll be a tearful laying out of history:
clandestine desire?   But the heroine has flown to the
moors, her lover thinking half-heartedly of a business in
snuff outside the city.   What I'd elected to expect met
every requirement.   So, where was I now?   This story –
no matter how many readings – develops into a conflict
between time zones.   I pick up the milk – the better to
start another new day.   Look, a wheel's come away in
my hand; her ladyship falls out: clouds of powder and
lace.   The story, seductive as it is, isn't enough to print.

FOR THE MOST PART

Hangman is a game for two, ludo for two or more.   There's
more violence in solitaire than I know how to handle.   As my
script here says 'Look down at the floor, say nothing' – there're
usually reasons for doing and not doing it.   Justice, too, has
its rules.   It throws around words as if their execution had
an infallible sense of exactness.   Am I to question that?   Is
complexity what these games are played for.   Metal puzzles I
soon get the hang of – there's a lot more to be said than ever
is said when the axe comes down, I reach for the dice, do I?

UNCONCERN

Do you remember that fountain we stood by during the
freak lightning show? Words off the page no less loud.
Can it be today's Times Atlas is heading at a rate of knots
for 1 : 1? Examples to consider: the man with a big hat
and a broken umbrella who struggles to pay his rent; voters
in an unnaturally even contest crying out for some barn-
storming new candidate; a yurt which proves more than
adequate when it's the simple life you're after – what else can
take the angst out of The News? What more do we know?
The fact our end game's playing itself out means I shall ask
less, but, at the same time, with the kind of intensity that
brings things to a head. Thud and blunder. Electricity,
sparks and flashbacks. To be followed by a hunger, not
only for how things were, but how they might be. As a
poetic, unworkable. Crime-of-the-Year will remind us
of the question. What in God's name *is* the question?
Don't know about you, but I'm out on just one spiral arm
of an average galaxy, bathed in light: poetics don't come
out of a vacuum any more than I'll be on a convoy to the
front or you'll be, as the cynics put it, 'abolishing dreams.'

MISSING PERSONS

Is it possible to shore up declining levels of ingenuity?   And would you want to?   The campaign for off-limits investigation is itself under investigation.   You can't accept hints or tokens from high street chuggers or Sunday abolitionists.   The misunderstandings that can occur between you and the hotel receptionist over video usage are legion.   Good guys, by and large, speak a better kind of English, but a Superman outfit does *not* a gallant make.   So, to get out there and build an appropriate relationship – not just with plutocrats, but with emissaries from failing states – is of more use to you than a three-piece suit and matching tie from some sub-Savile Row tailor the media's taken on board.   No, I've never carried a full set of The Verities, but I do have ports to go to in a storm.

THROWING THE JAVELIN

Libertines do it with flair.   Pre-Socratic philosophers made it a field sport under the stars – that way natural justice was like 'Wish You Were Here' or a daily postcard with blue dreams and updates on the sun.   I speak as a half-qualified free spirit in some things and as a wearer of brown sandals (note the heel strap).   I've spent so much time falling out with the world, a spell in fairyland sounds right.   Penchants and soft spots apart, a good half of every day is spent about a foot and a half away from what wise men call 'the wall' – the screen is nothing more than a sentence: by and by, you get to the end of it.   The point is to make a mark or the judges (anonymous) won't register the throw.   It's pikestaff-plain, I need to get out more, but what if you drop me a line?

SHEER ARTISTRY

for David Miller

There's a stone with hieroglyphics on it, but I can't read them;
there's a virtually indescribable rhythm in the background,
and I cannot identify the source. Of the resting on minimal
laurels there's absolutely no end, but look who's counting his
chickens. All the same, I'm determined to communicate
what's so great about inevitability. Endless, mad experiment
doesn't thrill me – even canticles fail to whip up anything in
the way of private frenzy. All right, I put myself about the
pigeons, that much is clear, but .... with the motorway now
buzzing in one ear and Sun Kil Moon in the other, I'm not for
clapping; what makes my future is an honest claret and the
entirely other blueness of the sky. It doesn't appeal to you?

PRIAPIC LIBERTIES

Don't tell me. There are painters and writers with fewer inhibitions than there are polemicists with too many. A subsuming of base material into gold, thereby depriving it of value and inconveniencing nobody. It seems (likely as we are to grovel in poetry to invaluable ends) they put mavericks in charge of not just the country, but nuclear reactors, missiles and 'the positive contribution of culture'. Are you happy, I am? – the outcome of years behind the wheel of chaos and candidates who never get in. I used not to care for righteous anger – endings being so often worse than beginnings. The inks I use now come in 'cartridges'. Does that change things, the word's not new?

SOMETHING HAPPENING?

An agency to turn poets into bespoke speculators and articles of the faith.   Reservations contain not outlaws, but the harvesters of such quaint truths, no-one can remember if they really knew them (such has been surface erosion and general grinding down).   Do I stop playing CDs and looking at paintings of dark tunnels in the eye?   Gastropubs and open planning can be awash with gabble or hush.   Sip slowly, quietly, let the lists grow longer.   Uranium, plutonium, waste products and speakers on the need to vote and how you should cast it.   The meadow you're standing in is wide open and dug under; a bulb without a shade says who we are. Somewhere we are neither a story nor a bite of refreshment.

BOTHERATION AND OTHER WORDS HE SAID

'Rather than duck out of a close encounter, I'm booked on the
next mission to 'full consciousness' and you know what that
means. 'Drat' wasn't the first word I said when told space
junk had become so common, collisions couldn't be avoided.
Minimal entry qualifications?   Enter the appropriate code
and trust in the first trajectory you thought of.   Rolling dice
and building platforms have about as much in common with
discovering new worlds as debunking a dastardly poetics.   I
was here on a scabby grant, counting everybody's falling star.'

LURES

Philosophers dream of flick knives, historians of catapults.
A diagram like a Venn will keep some of us in the loop,
while leaving others to icy winds and the wolves of the city.
I tremble, but I refuse to gasp: everything, as my tutor told
me, in moderation.   What we do about estrangement,
though, simply has to matter.   One way to get the hang
of it, is to skip parts 1, 2, 3 and go straight to episode the
last where the troopship's already bringing men ashore.
Some are scarred and battered, others walk off unaided, as
if they're back from a cruise (I'm not forgetting loners
out there in the wilderness).   For me, intersections are
superior – you get to meet like and unalike and say hello.

Two

A BROKEN ANGEL
OR A BUNDLE OF STRAWS

SPEECH BUBBLES AND EXPLICIT VERSE

for Rupert and Sue Loydell

Democracy would be a fine thing, but will I hear about it?

Cars overturn on bends, cats fall from trees and zero hours
contracts do whatever they can to be the good guy, even
as you bother to read them and struggle to focus.   If your

eyes are anything like mine, you'll be prone to 'incidents'.
Knowing when to turn up or – if you've created sufficient
havoc – collect your cards, doesn't always make it to print.

You have a cool eye – then you'll be quick to react?   Over-
come by kindness one minute, disregarded the next, links
us to happenings around the cosmos – an asteroid on the

loose will create frissons whenever we're told to look up.
So I shan't be saying much.   Security staff are warning of
problematics.   To put it another way, seeing clearly and

going public is living proof: I won't be falling on all fours.

MY INCONSTANT COMPASS

It was all about rats, gold, sable & ordure.   It was long, long

ago and I was rejecting not just one but a hundred theories.
So downright systematic, I'd collected just about everything
and knew where nothing was that didn't really matter.   Not

so much a favour asked for or given – more a by-product of
something like a séance.   Translucent as anything you saw
in the womb, touchable as the space where whatever you'd

been observing had stood.   The man said, get away; I said,
it's not a game you know and he looked away as I trowelled
into the pit.   For new bones, and a sky by night; oh, please.

Like treasure or annuities.   A good thing we saved the best.

CAKEWALKING HOME

Split me the difference?   Maybe we'll forget tomorrow,
think back to how reprocessing a cycle gave rise

to bland concessions.   Undone, but glad to be alive,
I'm sleeping rough – swallowing all the contradictions.

It doesn't have to be now – you can post the cheque
whenever: a leaden sky today may be cobalt tomorrow.

But, then, I couldn't be more averse to prophecy.
Besides, will I know it when it's here?   Quote: the time

of our lives!   Philosophers and homeopaths are but
murmurations on the skyline, while 'universal certainty'

is symptomatic of a night spent kicking up your
heels.   All's well if you say so i.e. if you really mean it.

LIKE A BOOK LIKE AN ISLAND   *for Ralph Hawkins*

It's only to be expected – never in any real sense

(nor can it be) what it seems.   The book like the
island has its edges: you can stand and look way
way out, but you need an accomplice, you really

do.   Personally, I wouldn't set off without one –
without a narrative that holds water or displaces
same.   Mischief today occupies a notable place

in the handling of a theme.   If not in sight, then
it's better you make it up.   One bloody hell of
a walk to the water + time equals extra.   By my

own calculation, we can be gone by 9 in the mor-
ning.   Whatever's in mind, I will not say no to.
Trust me and my crime-of-the-year poetic – any

old sea-bird pulled from the hat ends up a hero.
Being here is all that matters.   Even the ripples
look fancy.   Say 'hi' to your shipmate, and take

a peek at that compass – it's spinning like a top!

ANXIETY CHANGES NOTHING

At home & in the office, a file is a file is a file – you don't go

blanking an intern, so why blank the messenger?   Therapy
is available in coffee houses, melodrama at the Dog & Duck.
He knew that, one day, he'd spend twenty lifetimes on 'The

Stamboul Train', while stupidly rejecting larks in the picture
house.   She kept on counting; he looked, listened &, hours
later, came to.   In our hands here they are: the papers that

failed to redress a wrong, a million miles from the holding
centre.   She looked one way, he wrote off the other.   Hot
metal, steam; incremental mischief lay at the bottom of the

scale.   Where adultery connives with the clock on the wall.

NATURALLY UNPLUGGED

I'd give anything for access to bliss: 8 years fronting real-
time rockumentaries, with neither sponsor nor roadie,
is quite enough: doctors aren't ready to diagnose 'illness',

let alone ADHD – it says something about intimacy when
you immerse yourself in histology and end up in pieces.
Times to be had, believe me, before they get you, but if

your property's crashed, don't clap your hands – waiters
see signals as, well, 'faecal interregna'.   Vino nothing
but the 'medium mystical', for affairs of cash.   Scarcely

the heart.   In Calabria (pop. the last I heard c. 2 million),
regulars are blessed with sea on 2 sides & land reforms
that, with dollops of luck, will turn water into wine – yes,

you can tell we've been too long on the road: seeing us
do the quiet stuff, standards or something in the park.
Q: what's yours, still unverified & absent as a lark?   A:?

FOUR GOING ON FIVE

Years, however old you were when any and every ancien
régime collapsed, were the stuffed eternity you could

do without.   For April, it was the rudest month.   And
love, a broken angel or a bundle of straws, take your pick.

Care for a uniform made you more of a target, not less.

There was, by all means, the body on the parados, letters
to and fro.   The padre smiling – so careful is the word

for it – as you go.   Rule books, the subsequent set-to.
Art work still hanging on the wall, bottles, civilian blood.

INCORPORATE INCORPORATE

The centre left has a lot to do, the centre right has options

but can't tell which to take.   We're all in this to get some
and, asap, more – so why not wallow?   Unless I tighten it

up, the world & his wife will need to weave bad magic for
the rest – those without tribal affiliations they know of or

are 'prepared to criminalise'.   Such is the lingo, and such
is the pooling of dirty data.   Remember, I sold my house

to a paratrooper, valuables to the non-aligned.   Just one
of those days that goes awol; one for absentee regulators

to watch from half-baked corners in the sun – maxed out.
While dislocated here – in the meantime – my futures are

intermittent and off the wall.   Can you spell prescription?

MAYBE A BIT

but nothing remotely like this

Clouds know just what they're doing.   And my coffee has the
balance I hardly ever achieve.   Stranger than this, the area of sky
that's blue is visibly right for it – for everything we intend.

Beyond this, you can be (even be in the mood to be) over the
worst.   Lost, forgiven & right there in the mix.   I like the idea
of the girl sitting on the bookshop floor, reading The History

of Us & her friend beside her, untangling her hair.   Both of
them composing their now.   At once, it's different again and so
much other than we thought – as tricky, in fact, as a poem.

PLAUDITS ON A ROLL

Clauses within clauses, some love affairs within a stone's throw
of consummation, running out of steam.

Once, when they occupied the orangery, milady took umbrage.
It was not to be.   Taking flight

From that paragraph, she settled on another.   It was, short of
some miracle, no way to win a war, especially

One with a vengeance.   No limits beyond 32 lines, title and a
drop.   Steeling oneself against this writer

And her 'brute sensibilities' is as unthinkable as reimbursing a
burglar for his cut thumb.

Whatever chances existed of my meeting 'The Common Man'
foundered when I closed the book.

UNEQUAL MEASURE
for Peter and Pauline Dale

We saw him establishing a rapport.   Possessed as we were
of more than our fair share of travelogues, it was nothing to

find him 'somewhere' – his chosen themes: escapology and
Elizabethan sonnets.   I wouldn't treat any of this lightly – a

twist in the plot wants for nothing but deep thinking.   He
told me once about a distant life and how nymphs invaded

his privacy.   I sympathised and put him in touch with one
of our specialists.   It was every bit what he wanted and his

relationships bloomed like something exotic, like a journey
undertaken in another life: Thom. Wyatt bowled him over.

CHRONIC INDISPOSITION

Something tells me the disappearance was unintended.

'A concreted-over world can still be dug up', says time.
But, when owl calls to owl and never you, don't fly into

a rage.   Life merits less investigation than the woman
slumped over a wheel.   Her partner, the suspect in a

case already closed, is long gone on the costas.   Précis
your best thoughts, and, if you're satisfied, don't let on.

A warm sun is here to help, but it's no more than light
in a tunnel.   Consider that body in the lay-by.   Some-

one's last breath, a smouldering corpse?   'So business
is great', says the eye, 'and creation's as tabloid as you

make it'.   'A less than cheerful pronouncement', said
one in the crowd – 'the ultimate bomber on the moon'.

SWITCHING CHANNELS   *for Peter Hughes*

On a bad day, the only way to steal thunder is: pay the
price.   If we don't, they'll ask for reasons why.   Much

of East Anglia is history reclaimed: everything points to
Hunstanton or Orford Ness, throwing a light on many

things – does it black them out?   The first time, what-
ever she said and you said, proves wicked to translate.

Take the word 'peal'.   Its overtones go on & on.   On,
beyond caring, even (how long have we got?) beyond

hearing.   An hour when words get groped by sudden
light, when craftsmen, studiously, down tools.   How

far Rendlesham?   East is east, let's hear it for feelings,
the miraculous is on its way.   I say this hand on heart,

my Atlas of Chance hasn't ruled it out.   You get time
off for good behaviour.   Bell tower, lighthouse, mind?

IRREVERENCE

Priestess & madman – better suited to a violent chemistry

than an adolescent online, who can't see how nights out
can easily ruin a narrative & run up a storm.   I translate
'hindsight' as 'nightmare in the making'.   Having posed

questions about care and living it up, I don't expect – at
least on this watch – what straplines refer to as 'collateral
damage'.   Who wants contrarians sounding off?   Place

me in the spotlight and story is everything, never myself.
Crude truth, imagination making out in the dock.   If she
is mad for incense, he's for naked flame: love tickles pink.

As for appetite, it chews up the contents and spits us out.

ELBOW ROOM

i.m. Bernard and Malin Andrews

I come across so many unusual characters, so irregularly,
it's hard to think twice about meaning.

With ellipses and would-be cogencies like mine around,
you'd think there'd be much more

in the way of local damage?   When she scribbles those
marks of hers in grey over titanium white,

the sky lights up more intentions than even I believed I
had.   If the colour's not bright or bleeding,

I'll be hunting down others.   Consolation's a dab hand
at making pictures your own.   Look, I was so glad

to get your tip-off, I felt, even here in this secret location
(aka gallery), I could intervene.   The outlay?

Clearly huge, but, no, I couldn't refuse.   Reviewers may
be loathe to admit their non-attendance,

but other agents, kindly turned up and left notes.   *Girl
in a Tree, Fugitive Form, Time in an Unstirred Pool,*

Ice.   People and places you can't, in any dark equation
or through any pocket, afford to lose.   Some

of us package futures for you while you wait.   Others
dip a brush in water, ready to stain your mind.

PRE-PACKAGED, PREPAID

No time like now to reinforce a tradition.   Whether to be a
rep for half a hundred thesps or kick sand in the face of

adversity, some performances in the gym never worked out.
Paradise or success story or dismembered conversations

were as nothing to the parade of 'victims'.   Courtesy ruled.
But I did no better, stringing out time like 'Hiawatha' and

the first historic centrefold.   Top shelf, top gun, top of the
want lists, nobody cared.   Calling in favours or reacting

badly to comment sat unfavourably in the gods.   Play is
how any number of these worlds gets by, and, yes, me too.

IRREGULAR SEDUCTION

I pray for displacement, as I fret about loitering at the fire.

There's a memoir about me – no idea who wrote it.   Real
happenings occur on virgin land, with trees & lakes & the
long flowing hair of a maiden clothed in effects.   If I am
spirited away to the sound of music, the notes are never
those of a feeble ghostwriter or commissioner for oaths.
You know the one, it goes like this .... sometimes that's all

we can say.   No world is perfect, made in the likeness of
fools.   In any deliberation, permit external counsel.   Be
aware of spies indoors, troublemakers, quicker to digress
than a dagger is drawn & clowns, for the most part half-
asleep.   Back off before the virus bites, be a stay against
every containment.   Speak heedlessly as you're likely to.

She, being good, is also dangerous, you are what you are.

THE REVIVAL OF THE
INSPECTORATE FOR EVERYTHING

for Kevin Bailey

Such things approximate, in well read circles, to textual dark-
ness – think: *what did happen to the spider?*

On cue, it hits the floor – condensing facts into something
mute: with luck survivable.

But, whether it brokers a bloody deal, creates universal love
or gets higher scores on a desirability survey ....

Francis Bacon, begins as an interior decorator, says 'I'd like a
very, very ordered chaos', and maintains the discipline.

A lot rides on giving 'that without reality' the smirk of the mat-
erial – all shapes all shades, vertiginous pure colour.

Skip all that tosh about modelling clouds: for every big storm
or soul in torment, I've a shedful of u/s machinery.

Drop by if you're also forsaken – who knows, in awe of the
queen of hearts or, is it, a collapsible black square?

It's now or never – 'Alert Level 1' – people fall over, flames
engulf – nobody but nobody turns the page.

[extracts]

THINGS MOVE ON

With the gut defoliated – don't ask about antibiotics – you
can't spend every waking hour debating ends and means.
Commendable habits are seldom 24/7.   A moving lorry

presents no injunction to you or anyone to cross the road,
but sometimes you have to.   Place your emphasis; decide
on a strategy to kill and stick to it.   Illness, at certain times

and in certain places, is more or less the norm.   Not that
I'm missing out.   I have indiscipline on my side, hopefully
enough to shed a forensic light on mayhem: how to meet,

greet and wave it goodbye.   You can do it differently, it's
up to you, the choice for me is scary – the traffic's hardly
a gift to a man spending every second thought in dream.

TO THE DISMAY OF NONE

His first act was interrupted with the world on the point
of exploding.   Looking for provisos or protective

clothing was out of the question, maidservants scurried
here & there in the old familiar way, bosoms heaving

with anticipation.   It wasn't as though he didn't care –
he was more about his business than the photofit

leading light that sooner or later comes a cropper – the
stage lit up like someone given the best news ever &

prouder than maybe they ought to be of their position.
Down two steps & along the passage to a place of

correction?   Given a classical education was one thing.
Being blessed with a dozen cases of burgundy: that

was comprehensively taking the mick – from badinage
to spasms of modest disquiet, his mileage was low.

UNIVERSAL THEME PARK

If you're living in a 2-up, 2-down link house and don't get out
much, a prescription is needed to stop the rot and put x

portions of the exotic on your plate, maybe into your mind.
Tell me then, what you saw as ordinary wasn't a flight of green

parrots, a chicken in a basket, a cape daisy massively more
purple than love?   I believe you can live another life entirely

at a window: making paper decorations, writing letters about
how the paint dried, and so on.   New light dropping in

with scents of – you thought it forgotten, if not obliterated
entirely – a delicious yesterday you couldn't believe you lived

through.   But filled a vacuum in another world.   Reports of
'the good life' may be premature, but supermarkets are

still open, ready to fill you in.   Think about it.   If you don't
take my word for it, you'll be taking theirs.   Meanwhile …

look on Mary Fedden's or Winifred Nicholson's window sills
and live.   Throw back the shutters, get a significant lungful.

CREDO

The less I aim the more I hit my target, I said to a couple
of strangers I'd had words with at the baker's, while

rain poured down and reflections got the better of me.
If they were in it for wise words, well, it didn't show.

One shuffled his feet, the other blinked repeatedly. A
good sprawl, I intimated, is nothing if not to savour.

Behold, the end of the world and how to accomplish it.
I tell you straight, I promise nothing from this day on,

but to smack intellect from pillar to post, then sniff out
the opposition – that's the way to do it, they chimed.

HARRY, FOR WANT OF A BETTER NAME

You ask for a reference.   So I'll give you one.   A tiny spider
without a name is a regular on the study ceiling.   Moving,

mostly not at all or with irregular fits and starts.   I believe it
jumps, in fact, I've seen it.   Accents round the house: blue

glass, yellow pot, a lime green tiger – none of them foreign.
Early in the morning as I came by, I was overthinking: about

ideas of compassion – about people finding the time for it.
What time of day they'd choose, etc.   About 'ideas-over-

compassion'; why it is places burn and crumble.   At times
like these, when we're speaking English, pretty much (after

a fashion!), thinking nothing of it and why, first rain slaps
the windscreen.   The mind is off again: the value we place

on bruised and broken things.   I'm happy with that, and
wonder – how to sleep at night, head facing west.   As for

the prevailing entities?   They're not trading in names!   If
they were, wouldn't we know our home – every tiny word

that fits there?   Who in the night gets asked to jump?   I
refuse to guess.   Linnaeus went for anything with being.

DISBELIEF

It's the night of the damned and first day of Spring – a sky of

black horses.   Apocalypse, with lights that can never go out,
unless I say so/dream so.   Every last line sets up an ending,
then a new line.   You repeat & remember, spill the words a

little, not once believe they are yours.   Being innocent and
guilty, *they never were* & didn't know it, speak no language
but their own.   Mr Rat runs hotfoot to a hole in the corner,

an angel flies higher than intended, ready to break loose.   I
have witnessed nothing that hasn't seen the like & think it
more or less time to call us home – call everything to a halt.

Re-read the text, its shifty alibi and vindication.   Such sighs.

ONE ON ONE AT ELEVEN

The luxury of an 'I' is identical with an accident in the fast lane
or, come to think of it, a cold espresso served with/without.

A smile is all she takes, of course, I'm happy enough and do so.
Knowing it's me today – though I wish I was someone, even

anyone, else – and consistently can't be.   Let's speak, instead,
about flavour and an extraordinary absence/essence in the

world.   We might wish for nothing, but nothing can stop her
driving lickety-split.   It takes an accident to know the road.

FOR A SMALL CANVAS, FOR TODAY   *for Peter Riley*

Some red flowers take any amount of watering.
It looks like an arid landscape.   North Africa?
I have come down on the side of the locals,
no surprises waiting there as far as I can tell, but
they look right, I mean appropriate.
Comfortable with the situation confronting us.
I relish a valley, a rocky road down to a stream.

Off-canvas, it's a while before I get my bearings.
The gallery is a quality space, my mind is, to
all intents and purposes (regrettably), mined.
The girl with the withered arm is gracious,
accepting my flowers.   She will not look back.
I have put work in.   It is something to be
on a mission.   Things will recover, won't they?

ALL THE LONG WHILE

Some speak of high-end decoration, others of techno and
dub.   Mind renovation might be described, creatively, as
a semi-delinquent gig.   I'm at home with rock star myth,
but are you?   If there's hope for the devil, there's nothing

on the cards for labours of love: years in the eye of a good
storm don't mean a business can be turned around – I'd
explained that the hotel room was 'like that' on our arrival.
It was like handing security a shakeable, stuffed bear or a

game with no rules.   Lighting, cage & a monstrous bank
of souped-up amplifiers can articulate the unthinkable – if
you've nothing better to do, imply there's money to burn.
It's one crazy move, but look how they love it – a roomful

of fresh-faced clerks and shelf-stackers, can in hand, is yet
another.   Such a turn of events!   That 'justice' you kept
on about won back fame & fortune via a superannuated
discography of the 'new dead'.   Chaucer riding solemnly

into Canterbury, like someone under no illusion, saw each
blank wall as a load of bricks, then rewrote them.   As the
pardoner opined, and pithily, that's how you do it.   The
'human condition' amounts to what – uncontainable fire?

PHEROMONES AS WE KNOW THEM

Are really unreliable.   Breathing new life into a system,
any system, is like tarting up an ancient ruin

and putting it on the slate.   Crises misappropriate
the invaluable.   As ever I find myself at the back

of the queue.   It's a *rara avis* that doesn't, sooner
or later, run out of sky.   The poor man's lament

is a reformer's bread-and-butter.   Don't imagine
you're the one – kingmaker as well as bottle washer.

There's no easy way out of a bank vault I know of,
without sharing the risk.   You mix the worst with

a bit of the average, then give it a glitzy name.
Somebody it's hard to believe in is in a state to buy it.

EQUIVALENCE, DALLIANCE AND THE NUMBER 19

for Tim Allen

1

Clean slates, Battersea and a bumpy ride make it as hard to
draw the imagination as haunt a metaphor.

Processes that extend the supernatural into an unreadable
quotation create an identity you cannot bottle.

I address my guardians the way I was taught: de-gaussing
lends itself to both VDU & whoever looks on.

Capital Q is for Quality, small errors make fine judgements,
the bill is as clear as its meaning.

To speak of accomplishment, weed out mischief &, sighing
greatly, cherish the good bits Faust forgot.

2

Posthumous & blacker than comedy, is the last award and,
of course, the first time you hear it.

Polonium nearly had a son-in-law – committed to the des-
tination of facts that fled the country.

Whenever eyes grow moist or weary, under no known cir-
cumstances take holy orders.

The right bus for the right side of my brain will be as good
as it gets, if I can find or you can picture my pass.

Upstairs is where we happen – new stars & run-of-the-mill
supernovae, happy to be hanging up clues.

FOR SACRIFICE

As a child I had to slay dragons, even as my future fell into
arrears.   Henry sent letters beseeching her, I was in some
sort of coma, envying heroes and struggling with a quill.

'Don't tell me what to do with my money.'   Press now for
a pause and love at all costs.   She prayed for a long hot
Summer, suitors & a floral divan.   Wherever I am, I'm a

migrant wanting elsewhere.   Climbing ten foot fences or
making a case for a business in last orders, doing kings
proud.   She was bewitched by no-one, time smouldered.

CONSIDERING A POSITION

The Monument is where the fire started.   Imagine being on
that platform the time it broke out.   And caught in the rush

to take it down.   Reporter's notebook, heatproof pen, inks
and powers of deduction.   Though which way they decided

on, let alone which way – help – took our fancy, is very much
a game of soldiers.   I took a wrong turning – that's for sure.

Ashes retain heat, sparks fly; things last in the mind.   While,
for the folk that missed them, there's always *nostalgie de la*

boue.   French booze mostly.   Also the chance to bury the
last of your inhibitions: see what Masters of the Art knocked

up and back – remembering how the worst of us died down.
Here's to looking forward, chucking metaphors at the wind.

THE PACE IS PICKING UP

The estate is going bankrupt and processes, proud
and haughty, are, likely as not, for the chop.   Education
has – no-one's admitting it – twinges of regret.

Grandfather's portrait would hang on the wall, but,
instead, decides to keep its secrets.   Out of respect for
the kind of decay that opens a restaurant one minute

and closes it the next.   On account of nothing so weird
as maggoty fruit and a waiter who died in action
and refused every heart-rending request to come back.

Would that 'The Pleasure Factory' had hung on just
a little bit longer, but neither the City nor the clientele
chose to intervene.   Learning creeps up slowly on

the wisest.   The unlikeliest, with a hell of an artistic
flourish, put distance between the UPVC front door and
what – still no-one's sussed it out – goes on inside.

PLACES OF ENGAGEMENT   *for Steve Spence*

Beachcombing for one, another is a schoolroom with a folding

screen.   The poet in the next room paints a skull and cross-
bones on every tall cupboard and tells us, you take the blame.

You can pick up useful tricks like how not to or get clowns to
seek help.   Where everything is leading, there are as many

manuals as floorboards.   Most of them squeal if you apply
the pressure.   Clapboard holds everything together, whether

or not the committee care.   I'm a pirate & nobody knows it,
he says.   There is steel in his teeth, a rashness that rhymes.

It's for storms to be lovestruck and goodwill to run up the flag.

SENSORY KNOW-HOW   *for Tony Lopez*

The answer wasn't everything – it appears that, even before it
arrived, you knew more than you should.

The closer I am to a swollen river, the less need I have to swim.
Composure in my time suffers overmuch from thinking.

For risk is a plaything, it goes without saying – without asking
for advice or guessing why tomorrow on the calendar

is all white squares.   If you're sweating at the thought of it, it
may be a good idea to stay in.

Does this nerve cell [he points] know what it's trafficking?   I
see another child building towers – all of them leaning,

with nothing in her mind about Pisa, St Bridget's or the Angel
of Inclination.   There's nothing but bog between

political prejudice and the maths of money.   How this world
might long for Marthe out of the bath and

into real light isn't for thinking, but yearning remains one of
the few lights not to go out.

THE HOUSE OF USED CARDS

I was as distressed as anybody who could not be.   Which is

going some.   The hour wasn't – you could dissemble, say
you were the original stranger, the one with terrifying gaps
in his memory – against it.   All returns to finders had to be

actioned.   Tidied and dressed up – another treaty, the like
of which I'd never before witnessed, was drawn up, signed
and sent to the front.   Armies, suppliers and such were

invisible.   Metaphorical dogs that barked, that set fire to
words both on and off the page.   Walls, do you think back
to them, often, like me?   The matters of wonder – ivy-clad,

graffitied, or both – they would be coming down.   I took
my cue from a bookmaker pal, sat down and rewrote the
history of a planet, its procession of guilt and finery – see:

'Notes' in the margin, totally absent – they didn't read well.

SHIFTING A PERSPECTIVE   *for Tony Frazer*

Never a boat more half-full.   Excuse us, then, if we dive into
the lustrous, whipped up blue: out of a rock face,
into a jeweller's scales, if you don't mind hyperbole.   Things

come so quickly to the surface, there's scarcely time to review
the options.   In a 12th Cent. Chinese kind of way,
you can involve yourself in as large a world as you wish with-

out straying too far from home waters.   If the sail has inter-
mittently, a mind of its own, don't imagine there's
the faintest chance you'll be lost at sea.   'Dislocation' is the

shadow blotting out maps of an awful past.   Go easy on the
scope of it, attend to the symmetry of straight joy.
We dream it, even as we steal it, our attachments fill the sail.

ALPHABET INFORMATICS

Mulling over a Life decides some things, but declines much
more.   I was there when the tiger won his freedom and the

doves of peace were deselected.   You know it's a high-risk
business when the roar gets into your ears and thinking flies

out the window.   A for artisans, B for belladonna, C for the
kindest cut of all and so on: everything you can think of has

its story, tells it like 'I am' (there are rhymes here, if you look
hard, but a songbird sounds sweeter).   I didn't want to be

superimposed over a picture of anything, because nothing
looks like I am, and these words weren't much better, see if

they aren't.   Super-powers prowl around, monitoring all I
do.   If they've a clue what I'm up to, look at the state of us.

WHAT IF LIFE WERE TO CONSENT? (CONTINUED)

for Stevie Smith

Whatever next!   It's a long shot, really – you might get it
if you wait.   First class your best bet, but not by much.

Predictability went right out the window – seeing who was
throwing it, right off the wall.   A welcome?

It wasn't.   Far from it, in a little copse a little to the north
of us on the ridge, where conceptual streams, so

I hear begin and perhaps flow down, there's a lot to think
about, also irrigation.   Machineries, oh various, dust

and politics, they're (who knows who listens) variously at
it, trying out worrisome, equally odd repeats.   Catch

the rebound, if you've a mind to.   Employ an exotic skill.
Vote therapeutic.   Einstein and Bernstein were bit

players by all accounts in this regular long-term world,
knowing what calmed the soul.   I mean … For

convalescence, dip your toe into the freezing, dark blue
waters.   Chuckle and give thanks.   So good of you

to – forgive the clichés, the shenanigans of my hand-me-
down and wild and woolly conundrums – come.

THE SHEER HELL OF IT

To manufacture more product than your neighbours have
room in the house for, keeps a dog awake at night.   Why

did fixing my bike account for more nervous energy than
I had to offer?   It wasn't ideal, that.   Being so innocent

of the world.   We may come in for less motion sickness,
now wristbands can be got for two medium-size packets

of paracetamol.   Outside and beyond the purview of her
contingent loyalties lies the equivalent of a car you know

you've spent far too much time tinkering with.   What we
considered the finishing line was birds migrating.   For a

charged particle to have significance, it needs to collide.
Can you imagine every egotist doing the world a favour?

BURNING CALORIES AND SO ON

Chemical events feature in one biography after another.

You keep your head down and say nothing much.
The average adult speaks lucre like a pro, but who's
taking care of business?   Fairs, fêtes and saucy
campaigns can all lift the lid on fortified disorders.

I was up there in my eyrie when the world fell in; a
look can change anybody's picture – like reading
invisible writing, can in one hand & methuselah in
the other.   Want to feel the backlash?   Go direct

to the suppliers & tell them your brain's already
popping.   A wind-up collider or a vade mecum.
Mind of its own.   But the way it's organised, they
rebrand whatever's surplus, then sit back for year-

on-year growth.   A dedicated 'patient' can track
his/her progress on-line.   If a work-out leaves
them sweating, one evening shuffling readies will
put them ahead of the game.   Looking the real

deal's paramount if you're selling souls or lighting up.

Lightning Source UK Ltd.
Milton Keynes UK
UKHW041949180319

339393UK00001B/23/P